When You Struggle in the Spiritual Life

When You Struggle in the Spiritual Life

An Ignatian Path to Freedom

Timothy M. Gallagher, OMV

A Crossroad Book
The Crossroad Publishing Company
New York

The Crossroad Publishing Company
www.CrossroadPublishing.com

© 2021 by Timothy M. Gallagher, OMV

Book design by Tim Holtz
Cover Design by George Foster

Library of Congress Cataloging-in-Publication Data
Available upon request.

Books published by The Crossroad Publishing Company may be purchased at special quantity discount rates for classes and institutional use. For information, please email sales@CrossroadPublishing.com.

Contents

Acknowledgments

I am grateful to my editor, Roy Carlisle, who proposed a book on Ignatius's second rule; without his insight, this book would never have existed. I thank Gwendolin Herder of Crossroad Publishing for immediately welcoming this project and supporting its publication. Finally, I thank Emily Wichland for her dedicated and competent assistance in turning the manuscript into a finished book.

Introduction

This book is for all who love the Lord, who seek to grow in that love—and who struggle. One who seeks God, who at times, perhaps often, feels weak and confused but who sincerely seeks God: this is the person to whom St. Ignatius speaks.

Some years ago, I wrote a book of personal reflections on St. Ignatius of Loyola's fourteen rules for discernment.[1] When my editor read the chapter on the second rule, he commented that this might stand on its own as a book. I never forgot his suggestion, and it led to the book that you are now reading. In it, I re-present that chapter with the adaptations suggested by a separate publication.

What Are St. Ignatius's Rules for Discernment?

We all experience an ebb and flow in our spiritual
lives. At times, we are filled with spiritual energy.
Prayer is alive. We sense God's closeness. We look
forward to the Eucharist. We explore new steps
to grow spiritually.

At other times, and for reasons we may not
understand, that energy seems to fade. Then
prayer is difficult. It is hard even to want to pray,
and we may pray less. God does not feel close.
Church activities no longer attract us. Those new
steps that in another time seemed so inviting, now
draw us less. Who of us does not know such times?

Ignatius first became aware of such experiences
during his convalescence from injuries received
in battle. Until the age of thirty, his life had been
far from God. Now, as the slow days of healing
passed, he began to note the response in his heart
to thoughts of living in two very different ways:
one worldly, the other dedicated to God. In the
first case, initial enthusiasm consistently turned
to emptiness; in the second, initial enthusiasm

2

constantly led to joy. This new awareness forever changed his life. It was the first step on a path that led to sanctity and great fruitfulness in the Church and in the world.

Marveling at these patterns in himself, he pondered their meaning. As he did so, and as prayer, reflection, and further experience shed further light upon this ebb and flow, Ignatius formulated his fourteen rules—practical guidelines—to help us understand and navigate this same experience.[2] He crafted these rules in his classic *Spiritual Exercises*, a manual for a retreat experience of thirty days. For five hundred years, these rules have blessed men and women who love the Lord, and today their radius is wider than ever.

As with Ignatius, much changes in our spiritual lives when we understand these alternations and know how to respond to them. For forty years now, I have seen Ignatius's rules bring light and hope to faithful people. I have seen his rules set people free from discouragement, and free to love and serve the Lord.

Why a Book on Rule 2?

My editor intuited well that Ignatius's second rule is fundamental to the spiritual life. In rule 2, Ignatius clarifies what we all experience when we seek to grow toward God: the encouraging action of the good spirit and the discouraging lies of the enemy. I have seen this rule change lives. When we understand that these disheartening lies *are not of God* but of the enemy, they no longer harm us, and we are set free to love the Lord. As I present Ignatius's rules, people often say, "Everyone should know this!" I share that conviction.

In this book, we will explore Ignatius's second rule and review examples of this rule in practice. I also share my own experience of rule 2 and how it has blessed my life. I share this because, as will be apparent, it is so ordinary and so like the experience of many. My circumstances—religious and priest, engaged in specific ministries—are individual, as are my story and personality. But my experience of the rules is, I believe, like that of any

person, in any circumstances—layperson; single
or married; active in business, at home, or in the
Church; religious woman, deacon, or priest—who
seeks to live the Christian life. Servant of God
Dorothy Day affirms that "you write about yourself because in the long run all man's problems are
the same."[3]

To provide the context for rule 2 and also the
text of other rules referenced, I have added two
appendices. Both contain the entire set of fourteen rules. In the first appendix, I provide a lit-
eral translation of Ignatius's original Spanish text.
In the second, I render his text in more brief and
contemporary language. I first composed this ver-
sion for university students. When I posted it on
social media, I found that it was widely welcomed
beyond that audience. I include it here for any
who may find it helpful.

This book may be read individually or with
a group. The reflection questions at the end
of chapters 3 and 4 will assist in both settings.
For those who wish to pursue Ignatius's rules

further, I provide additional resources at the end of this book.

May Ignatius's wisdom provide hope and renewed energy on the spiritual journey.

Rule 2 of St. Ignatius's Fourteen Rules for the Discernment of Spirits: The Text

In persons who are going on intensely purifying their sins and rising from good to better in the service of God our Lord, the method is contrary to that in the first rule. For then it is proper to the evil spirit to bite, sadden, and place obstacles, disquieting with false reasons, so that the person may not go forward. And it is proper to the good spirit to give courage and strength, consolations, tears, inspirations and quiet, easing and taking away all obstacles, so that the person may go forward in doing good.

CHAPTER 1

The Setting of the Text

God wishes us to know that he keeps us
safe all the time, in sorrow and in joy.
  Julian of Norwich, *Revelations of Divine Love*

Who can say how many thoughts pass through our minds in the day? How many stirrings of joy, sadness, hope, and anxiety we feel? This interior experience affects our spiritual lives in significant ways. Ignatius formulated his fourteen rules to help us become aware of such experience, understand what is of God and not of God in it, and know how to respond to it.

In his rules, Ignatius clarifies how both the enemy and the good spirit work. By *enemy* he intends Satan and his associated fallen angels; the wound of concupiscence—that legacy of original sin that, unless resisted, will pull us away from God; and spiritually harmful influences in the world around us. By *good spirit* he intends God himself, the Holy Spirit; the good angels; the gifts given in baptism—the indwelling of the Holy Trinity, sanctifying grace, the theological virtues, all the other virtues, the gifts of the Holy Spirit, and individual charisms; and, finally, all spiritually helpful influences around us in the world.

These are not equal actors! The first is a fallen creature—yes, of a higher order than we, but still no more than a fallen creature; the second is the eternal, omnipotent, and infinitely loving God. Both are real. Both act. Both must be understood. But they are not equal. Ignatius's rules, as a result, offer great hope and confidence.

The second rule, our focus in this book, forms a pair with the first. In these two rules, Ignatius explains how the enemy and good spirit work in a person depending on that person's spiritual situation.

If a person is living in confirmed serious sin, how will the enemy and how will the good spirit work? Ignatius addresses this question in the first rule.[4] In such persons, he says, the enemy works in the imagination, presenting images of sensual pleasures. With the imagination so filled, the person is likely to continue on this path, as the enemy desires. The good spirit, on the contrary, will sting and bite in the person's conscience such that, if the person is open to this troubling action, he or she will reject the life of sin and return to God, our one true source of happiness.

When, however, a person loves God, seeks to live according to his word, and desires to grow closer to God, how will the enemy and how will the good spirit work? Ignatius answers this question in his second rule. If you are reading this book, most likely this is your spiritual situation and your desire. You will, therefore, find nothing abstract in this second rule. Ignatius will be speaking directly to you. Like so many in the past five hundred years, you will find that he understands your experience, articulates it clearly, and points the way forward.

The subsequent rules presuppose the person of the second rule. In them, Ignatius explains spiritual consolation (joyful stirrings of the heart in the spiritual life) and spiritual desolation (heavy stirrings of the heart in the spiritual life) and then supplies a wealth of spiritual tools for responding to both.

But first we need to understand the second rule. In those who sincerely seek God, Ignatius says, the enemy will employ four tactics and the good spirit, five. These tactics are the topic of the second rule and of this book.

CHAPTER 2

**The Person:
One Growing toward God**

I felt myself renewed to my very depths by
Him, ready for a new life, for duty, for the
work intended by His providence. I gave
myself without reserve, and I gave Him
the future.

Servant of God Élisabeth Leseur,
My Spirit Rejoices

Ignatius's second rule is the following:

Second Rule. The second: In persons who are
going on intensely purifying their sins and
rising from good to better in the service of

God our Lord, the method is contrary to that in the first rule. For then it is proper to the evil spirit to bite, sadden, and place obstacles, disquieting with false reasons, so that the person may not go forward. And it is proper to the good spirit to give courage and strength, consolations, tears, inspirations and quiet, easing and taking away all obstacles, so that the person may go forward in doing good.[5]

In this rule, Ignatius speaks to all who love God and desire to grow closer to him. He describes this situation according to two complementary qualities: such persons are "going on intensely purifying their sins" and simultaneously "rising from good to better in the service of God our Lord." These people are energetically seeking freedom from sin and likewise growing in God's service— they are actively pursuing new steps to love and serve God more fully. An example will concretize the spiritual profile Ignatius intends in this rule.

Peter's Experience

Peter is a fifty-three-year-old married man and father of three children. He was raised Catholic and, apart from a few years in college, has always practiced his faith. For him, this means attending Sunday Mass, ensuring that his children receive the sacraments, and praying on occasion.

One Sunday, as Mass was ending, the pastor announced a parish retreat and warmly invited his parishioners to attend. The retreat would be held in a local retreat house during the coming Lent. Peter had never made a retreat, and the thought of a weekend with talks on the faith, times of prayer, and space for quiet appealed to him. That evening, he spoke with his wife, who encouraged him to attend. Peter registered for the retreat and looked forward to the experience.

When the weekend arrived, Peter found the talks engaging and the times of prayer fruitful. On Saturday evening, he took part in the penance service with preparation in common and individual confession following. Peter decided to receive the sacrament and approached one of the priests, who received him with goodness and understanding. Peter generally went to confession before Christmas and Easter, but this was different. The talks, the quiet, and the prayer prepared him for a deeper experience of the sacrament.

Peter shared with the priest his new awareness of habits that were not spiritually good for him: ways of using the internet and television that diminished his spiritual energy; kinds of conversation into which he had drifted and that he now saw were harmful; practices at work that skirted moral boundaries; a slowness to assist his wife and children when this conflicted with his own interests.

Peter spoke openly of this to the priest and found the priest's response helpful. His words lifted Peter's heart and helped him experience God's love, mercy, and forgiveness. As he left the confessional, Peter felt a deep peace he had long sought.

That evening, Peter walked on the grounds of the retreat house. His heart was filled with a quiet joy. He found himself desiring to begin a new spiritual journey. Peter resolved that he would go to confession regularly, and after the retreat did so. He changed his use of the internet and television, eliminating the harmful practices. Unobtrusively, Peter distanced himself from the destructive conversations and questionable business practices. He strove to overcome the self-centeredness that limited his love for his wife and children. In Ignatius's terms, Peter is now a person who, with humble trust in God and diligent effort, is *going on intensely purifying his sins.*

As Peter did this, something else happened. He grew more patient with his children and more present to his wife. He was more cheerful at work and readier to assist others, who appreciated his new attentiveness to them.

During the retreat, Peter had learned of a men's group in the parish that met before work on Wednesday mornings. He joined the group and enjoyed the sharing and the talks. Some of the men went to daily Mass, and a few months later,

Peter also began attending Mass at times during the week. As the weeks passed, this practice grew more frequent. Peter's new interest in his faith encouraged similar steps in his wife, and a new spirit of faith and harmony gradually developed in their home. In Ignatius's terms, Peter is now a person who is *rising from good to better in the service of God our Lord.*

The Profile of Rule 2

Further examples might include the married woman who takes new steps to remove spiritual obstacles and to grow in prayer and service of the Lord in her family life; the young man who begins his seminary studies with energetic desire to grow in God's love and service; the single person who takes new steps in the spiritual life; the woman who enters a religious community and now seeks new closeness to the Lord and more faithful service; the priest who feels new spiritual desires, removes unhelpful practices from his life, and grows in dedication to his parishioners. In each case, the profile of rule 2 is present: these are people growing in freedom from sinfulness and rising in God's love and service.

In rule 2, Ignatius outlines *four basic tactics* of the *enemy* when seeking to *hinder* such persons' spiritual growth. He likewise names the *five basic tactics* of the *good spirit* in seeking to *facilitate* these persons' growth. Over the years, I have come to see this rule as fundamental. If people who love the Lord assimilate it well, they will find that they understand much of their spiritual experience and so know how to respond to it. We will examine first the tactics of the enemy and then those of the good spirit.

CHAPTER 3

Four Tactics of the Enemy

Haven't you tried before to improve and be better, and nothing came of it? So what is the use of trying anymore?

Leo Tolstoy, *Resurrection*

Ignatius names four tactics by which the enemy seeks to hinder the growth of such persons. The enemy, he says, will "*bite, sadden,* and *place obstacles, disquieting with false reasons.*" We will review each.

Biting

The enemy will attempt, Ignatius says, to *bite*—that is, to gnaw—at the peace and joy these progressing persons experience as they grow. Ignatius's word, the Spanish *morder*, expresses exactly this: a biting, gnawing action. In this way, the enemy seeks to weaken these persons' energy for growth, leading them to desist from further efforts.

This is a common tactic of the enemy. I see it often in my own experience, and I see it in others. It may present itself thus: "Yes, that (your prayer, your service of the Lord, your living of your vocation, your love of others, and so forth) went well, but . . ." The "but" may be followed by various forms of gnawing:

- "Yes, that went well, but why did it take you so long?"
- "Yes, that went well, but you pushed too hard."
- "Yes, you have grown in this area, but why didn't you address this before?"
- "Yes, that went well, but you could have done more."
- "Yes, you did that, but it won't last."

This "Yes . . . but . . . " dynamic may take these or similar forms. Such gnawing is not an incitement to sin but simply an attempt to diminish our spiritual energy. If we are not aware of this action of the enemy, it will burden us. If we are aware of it, name it for the biting of the enemy that it is, and reject it, our energy for spiritual growth will continue undiminished.

In a letter of spiritual direction, Ignatius writes that if the enemy "sees that . . . a person avoids not only all mortal sin and all venial sin (as much as the latter is possible, for we cannot avoid them all) but even tries to keep from himself the very appearance of slight sin, imperfection, and defect, he tries to darken and confuse that good conscience by suggesting sin where there is none, changing perfection into defect, his only purpose being to *harass and make one uneasy and miserable*. When, as frequently happens, he cannot induce one to sin, or even hope to do so, he tries at least to vex him."[6] *Harass*, make one who is growing *uneasy and miserable*, and, when he cannot induce this person to sin, at least to *vex* him: this perfectly describes the enemy's tactic of *biting*.

As is generally true in these rules, Ignatius writes from experience. After his conversion, Ignatius spent three days at the Benedictine abbey of Santa Maria de Montserrat, preparing and making a life-changing confession. Some months later, in a time of great spiritual growth, a thought began to trouble him regarding that confession. Ignatius recounts of himself: "Even though the general confession he had made in Montserrat had been made with great diligence and completely in writing, as has been said, nonetheless it seemed to him at times that he had not confessed some things, and this caused him much affliction."[7] In a time when Ignatius is "going on intensely purifying his sins" and "rising from good to better" in God's service, the enemy does not attempt immediately to lead him into sin but simply *bites* and gnaws at the peace Ignatius would otherwise feel in God.

Are we aware of this tactic of the enemy in our own experience? Do we name it and reject it?

Saddening

The enemy will also, Ignatius affirms, attempt to *sadden* the person who is rising spiritually. Peter, for example, experiences a quiet joy at the spiritual newness that has entered his life with new freedom from sinfulness, a livelier faith, and increased energy to love at home and in the workplace. A day comes, however, when he notes a diminishment of that joy. Now a film of sadness overlays his prayer, his involvement in the parish, and his efforts to love. Now his spiritual energy is dampened, and he no longer feels "any interior taste or relish" for the things of God.[8] Questions, perhaps imperfectly articulated but very much felt, may arise: "Why continue with all of this when there is no longer much joy in it? What is the value of all these efforts?"

If Peter is not aware of this tactic of the enemy and does not reject it, the sadness he feels may lead him to relinquish his efforts to "rise from good to better"—and such is the enemy's purpose. All who are growing in the Lord may well experience this tactic of the enemy.

Placing Obstacles

As Peter pursues spiritual growth, the enemy will attempt to *place obstacles* in his path. The same will be true of all who seek to progress in God's love and service.

When Augustine pursues freedom from his former life of sin, he tells us that "I was held back by mere trifles, the most paltry inanities, all my old attachments. They plucked at my garment of flesh and whispered, 'Are you going to dismiss us? From this moment we shall never be with you again, for ever and ever. From this moment you will never be allowed to do this thing or that, for evermore.'"[9] Lightly behind these whisperings are questions such as these: "You want to change? You want freedom from your sinfulness? How many times have you tried? How long has it ever lasted? What makes you think it will be any different this time? You know yourself. You know you are too weak. You know you cannot live without this."

Such is the enemy's tactic in persons seeking to rise spiritually: *obstacles, obstacles, obstacles*.

26

These persons, too, will hear the enemy's whisperings: "You are too weak. You can't do it. Why get your hopes up? Why make efforts that will go nowhere?" May I ask, have any of us heard such whisperings when we have desired to grow spiritually?

Nekhlyudov, the principal character in Tolstoy's novel *Resurrection*, desires to rise from the moral depths into which he has fallen. As he considers this step, he, too, experiences the enemy's obstacle-placing action: "'Haven't you tried before to improve and be better, and nothing came of it?' whispered the voice of the tempter within. 'So what is the use of trying anymore? You are not the only one—everyone's the same—life is like that,' whispered the voice."[10]

Gerald is a forty-one-year-old married man who, after twenty years away from the Church, has recently returned to the sacraments. For six months now he has faithfully attended Sunday Mass with his family and is making sincere efforts to overcome earlier patterns of sinfulness. He rejoices at the new peace he experiences and the new harmony in his family and at work.

Today Gerald is attending Sunday Mass. The Gospel is Luke 11:1–13, "Lord, teach us to pray." The priest gives a simple but heartfelt homily on prayer and invites his parishioners to consider spending ten minutes a day in prayer with the readings of the Mass for that day. As Gerald listens, he feels God's closeness, and his heart is warmed with gratitude to God for the goodness of what is happening in his life. A thought comes: "If simply praying once a week at Sunday Mass is already making this difference, what would happen if I did what Father is suggesting and prayed daily?" Further thoughts arise: "I could certainly arrange my morning to set aside ten minutes each day. And, actually, all I have to do is ask my wife for help, because she has been doing this for some years. She will be happy to show me how to find the readings and get started." Gerald resolves that he will speak with his wife that evening and will begin this practice the next morning.

The day continues with its various activities. At supper, a tension arises between Gerald and his teenage son, and it does not resolve well. This tension burdens Gerald's heart as the evening unfolds. Now the children are asleep, and Gerald is in his study, preparing for work the next morning. He remembers that he had planned to speak at this time with his wife about the ten minutes each day with Scripture.

But now his thoughts are different: "Who are you kidding? You've been away from the Church for twenty years, and look at the way you've lived. You've never even read Scripture. What makes you think you'll understand anything written there? Why approach your wife about a practice that is bound to fail? You'll just embarrass yourself and her. You had a nice experience at Mass this morning, but that doesn't change anything. It's not going to last." *Obstacles, obstacles, obstacles* . . . in the way of one who is seeking to rise from good to better in God's service.

Clearly, what happens next matters. If Gerald succumbs to the enemy's obstacle-placing action and does not speak with his wife that evening, what will his prayer look like a week later? A month? A year? Five years? But if, with spiritual awareness and courage, Gerald rejects this action of the enemy, holds firm to the grace of the Mass that morning, speaks with his wife, and begins the ten minutes of prayer the following morning, what will his prayer look like a week, a month, a year, and five years later? *Right here*, in the silence of this evening, Gerald will make a key decision regarding his spiritual growth. And *right here*, Ignatius wants to help us. Most of the spiritual life consists of precisely such situations and decisions—quiet, largely unseen, "small" decisions that shape our spiritual journey. The wisdom of the Ignatian rules—living the discerning life—can make all the difference.

Disquieting with False Reasons

That evening, the enemy may attempt a further tactic as well. He may seek to *disquiet* Gerald with *false reasons*. He may suggest *reasons* to desist from praying the ten minutes daily. Because he is "a liar and the father of lies" (Jn 8:44), these will be *false* reasons and will have a debilitating effect on Gerald's heart: they will *disquiet* him, diminishing his affective energy for growth.

The enemy may bring "reasons" such as these: "You want to begin daily prayer with Scripture? You know what this is really about? You've been getting nice feedback on your new spiritual journey, and you like the compliments. You want more of them. And you know what else is at work in this desire? You won't admit it, but you are competing with your wife. You want to be as spiritual as she is. And if you are really honest, you'll admit that you'd like the children to see you as even a little more spiritual than she." All these and similar "reasons" are false. None of this was present that Sunday morning at Mass but rather only a happy sense of God's closeness and of gratitude, with a desire to grow in the spiritual life. Yet if Gerald is not aware of this tactic of the enemy, these false reasons may well disquiet him and weaken his resolve to go forward.

I have seen this tactic of the enemy take various forms. When people grow in the spiritual life and in living their vocations, the enemy may whisper the following: "See, you were never authentic before." If they believe this lie, the joy of growth will be changed into disquiet of heart.

In times of spiritual progress, of newness in prayer, understanding, and service, questions like these may arise: "Why weren't you praying like this before? Why didn't you see this before? Why didn't you give yourself in service like this before? There's something wrong with you. You're so slow to take these steps." The truth is exactly the contrary: blessed and fruitful growth is occurring in these persons' lives. Again, if they believe these false reasonings, their hearts will be disquieted.

When the journey of growth involves struggle, a voice may be heard: "It's too late. Look at what you've done! Look at the way you've lived! You've marred things, and it can't be undone. You've failed in your efforts to love God, and now it's too late. It can't ever change." Or a slight variation of the same: "Look at you struggling. You're going backward in your spiritual life. It's all going to end badly."

In yet another way, the enemy may attempt to disquiet with false reasons. When people who love the Lord find thoughts and desires contrary to that love arise involuntarily in their hearts, they may be troubled: "See, look at you! You feel such desires. You think such thoughts. You are unworthy of closeness with God. You are a failure in the spiritual life. And you will never change."

John of the Cross speaks of *voluntary* thoughts and desires that *do* hinder spiritual growth and then, turning to the *involuntary* thoughts and desires that *do not*, continues:

> I am not speaking here of the other natural, involuntary appetites, or of thoughts that do

33

not pass beyond the first movements, or of other temptations in which there is no consent. These things do not give rise to any of the evils previously mentioned. Though the passion and disturbance they momentarily cause make it seem that one is being defiled and blinded, such is not the case; rather, they occasion the opposite good effects. Insofar as one resists them, one wins strength, purity, comfort, and many blessings, as our Lord told St. Paul: Virtue is made perfect in weakness [2 Cor 12:9].[11]

Natural, involuntary appetites . . . thoughts that do not pass beyond the first movements, or . . . other temptations in which there is no consent: to know that such are not sinful and that, on the contrary, *we grow* through resisting them, closes the door to many false reasons by which the enemy seeks to disquiet us. To banish the enemy's false accusations from such sensitive places of the heart awakens hope and energy for the journey.

The Hindering Tactics of the Enemy: Some Examples

I quote the following from my journals over the years. I offer them as representative, in one person's experience, of how these tactics of the enemy may present themselves in daily life.

"Three Ways of Biting in My Prayer"

From notes on a meeting of spiritual direction with Father Ed, my spiritual director for many years:

> Today Father Ed helped me to see three different ways in which the enemy "bites" at my peace when in prayer. With his help, I saw the following:
>
> When I feel drawn to spend quiet time in prayer, just with the Lord and without much mental activity, and find this nourishing and joyful, there is the voice that says, "You're not really praying. You should be doing more, reflecting on a scriptural passage, using the time better." This voice awakens a small sense

of uneasiness that weighs on my prayer. It is not clamorous; it just saps the joy. Because it is not clamorous, I don't easily see it.

When I want to share "small" things with the Lord, ask help in daily matters, or share daily concerns about work, relationships, projects, small tensions, and similar things, there is a voice that says, "With all the real problems in the world, people in the midst of wars and hunger, deep physical suffering, and lives torn apart, you should be ashamed to bring such small concerns to the Lord. With such great needs in the world, you are asking for help with these small burdens?" Father Ed quoted Jesus's words that even the hairs on our head are counted, that not a single sparrow falls to the ground without our Father knowing it (Lk 12:6–7). Everything in my life matters to God, and this hesitation that weighs on my freedom to share these things in prayer because they are so small is the enemy's biting. I should reject it.

Sometimes I remember the writings of spiritual figures like John of the Cross who say that many come to the threshold of deeper prayer, stop short, and never go further. When my prayer seems dry or difficult, after all these years, at times I think of those writings and wonder if I am not among these persons. This, too, awakens a quiet sense of burden, just a thread, not loud or in the forefront, yet it causes doubt and a little uneasiness. This, too, Father Ed says, is the enemy's biting and is to be rejected.

In such ways, we may experience this "biting" action of the enemy, quietly weakening the joy of the spiritual journey. It is blessed to see it and find freedom from it.

"You Could Have Done More"

I noted the following after some weeks of writing, when I was about to leave the parish that had hosted me and return to my community residence. The parish was near my family home, and I was there so that, while writing, I could also assist my mother. At that time, she was alone, in questionable health, and needed the family. The days, divided among parish, writing, and family, were intense and fruitful. I was to leave the next day.

I feel no energy to work today, and I must. There is packing to do and the car to get ready. Everything has to be in place so that I can leave tomorrow morning. I don't really know what I want. Probably it is to have my own work and life again. Maybe part of it is just the transition. It has not been easy to be here, and I miss my own setting.

There is some sense of guilt, since I haven't worked on the writing these past few days. Father Ed counseled against it, and I have found it helpful to take things more lightly. I have some energy back now. The decisions the family faces have taken so much energy.

I think there may be some plain spiritual desolation in this. In reality, things have gone well with the writing, and I've been able to help the family in important ways. The voice that accuses is harsh: both words, *accuse* and *harsh*, tell me something about which spirit is at work. The thoughts are: "You should have done more. You should have worked harder. You are not doing as much as others you know. You tell everyone that you've done a lot, but you know you could have done more."

The signs of the enemy are here: the accusations and the harshness. The truth is that I didn't work on the writing this past week because, though I tried, family issues took all my time and energy. Father Ed confirmed this when we spoke. Had I tried to write regardless in these circumstances, I would have finished this time utterly exhausted.

I think this is really what is bothering me: the enemy is at work in these accusations. I need simply to let them go.

I believe that when I wrote these words I was seeing clearly how the enemy, working in vulnerable spaces in my heart, was "biting" in regard to a time that had been rich relationally and fruitful in terms of writing. Describing this in the journal helped me see it more clearly still.

"I'll Slide into the End"

This next entry was written on the fifth day of a six-day preached retreat. Each day I gave two talks and met individually with retreatants. I can still see the room and desk at which I sat when writing in my journal. Objectively, the retreat was going well and the people were receptive. The vulnerable space was the tiredness that developed over the days and the sense of aloneness as I wrote:

> I can see various tactics of the enemy at this point in the retreat. The feeling that, with three talks to go, "I'm tired of this," with a heaviness of heart. When there were two

talks left, I felt a sense that "It's over," again with heaviness and lack of desire to give the remaining talks. From this same heavy space came the thought, "I don't want to 'pump out' another talk. It's gone well thus far; now I'll just slide into the end."

In such ways, I see the enemy's saddening action. Certainly, after five intense days of guiding a retreat, some physical and emotional weariness was natural. But the spiritually heavy and sad feelings described here were not objective and, unless rejected, would diminish my dedication and joy in this service.

"This Will Be a Long and Hard Road"

One way that I experience the enemy's obstacle-placing action is the sense that a new spiritual step I hope to take will be possible, yes, but only after many years of hard effort. The effect is to eliminate any hope of taking this step in the present or near future.

41

I suspect that I am not alone in this! This next entry summarizes Father Ed's advice after a meeting with him:

In everything, whatever burdens you carry, turn quickly to the Persons of the Trinity, to Mary, and ask for help. Reject the sense that "I can't do it, it will be unbearable, the future will go badly . . ." Turn to the Trinity and ask for help. They are eager to be with you and help you. Move from a stance in which you feel that you must make things happen, and open your heart to receive the grace and strength the Lord wants to give you as you do these things.

This is not hard to do. It is simple, easy. The enemy will place obstacles, make it seem that this is a huge shift, major, slow, hard; that this move from pushing to receiving requires a long and hard road. No, it is easy. You only have to ask and to receive. It can be done now.

"A Quiet, Soft Source of Worry"

The following is also from the weeks in the parish mentioned above, when I was writing and helping my mother. The pastor and I had agreed that I would say a daily Mass and otherwise be free for these further responsibilities. The weeks were fruitful, and I was grateful for them. One day, I noted troubling thoughts and a response to them:

Where there is fruitfulness, it seems that there will be an attack. The enemy's accusations are still there: "You rise earlier than the other priests. You are proud, competing with the pastor who also rises early. You are trying to impress the other priests." No, I'm just working at the rhythm that works best for me in periods of writing.

Again, "You are working hard, driving yourself, wearing yourself out. This is not what God wants. It's coming from you." No, after some weeks of writing, I feel good, am happy in the work, look forward to it, and

43

am maintaining a healthy pace in general. Yes, I could take breaks sooner at times, but this is very different from the enemy's lies. His way is to take a small thing and make a quiet, soft source of worry out of it.

Finally, "You aren't helping very much with Masses, when there is so much that could be done in the parish." This can lead me to live the days with an uneasy feeling. Again, the arrangement was clear, why I am here, and where my time should be spent.

I need this attention to the enemy's soft lies, low-key, quietly spoken, which can cause tribulation in the soul, lessening of peace, agitation that is not dramatic, just a touch of agitation.

All of this was, I believe, the enemy's attempt to disquiet with false reasons. The contrast of these disquieting thoughts with the richness of what was, in fact, happening was striking.

The Truth Will Set You Free

The pleasures the enemy proposes, Ignatius writes, are *apparent* (rule 1), and his reasons *false* (rule 2). Everything the enemy suggests is either an outright lie or the truth twisted in some way. People who love God and seek spiritual progress tell me how life-changing it is to realize that the voice that bites, saddens, places obstacles, and disquiets with false reasons *is not God's voice* but rather that of the enemy. This realization opens the path to freedom.

When those who are *growing toward God* (rule 2) confuse the biting, saddening, obstacle-placing, and disquieting action of the *enemy* with the stinging action of the *good spirit* in those *heading away from God* (rule 1)—a situation utterly different than their own—great pain results. When, that is, with good will but without the necessary spiritual formation, they believe that this troubling action of the enemy is actually the good spirit speaking the truth about their spiritual situation, discouragement follows. On the contrary, when they understand that this troubling action of the enemy is all a lie, that it is not God's word to them, that it does not define their spiritual identity, *they are on the path to freedom.* Then they know that this troubling action is to be rejected for the lie it is. This realization can be life-changing.

People have told me that when they felt this biting and disquieting action of the enemy, they thought it meant that *they were bad.* To know that they are not the authors of this experience, that it arises from another agent—the enemy— and that this is an ordinary experience on the spiritual journey brings great freedom. Then they can take steps to reject these tactics of the enemy.

Questions for Reflection

Review your experience of the enemy's four tactics, and with the Lord, prepare to name and reject them in your daily life:

What discourages you in your spiritual life? How would you describe the biting tactic of the enemy in your experience?

How have you experienced the "Yes . . . but . . . " tactic of the enemy? What form does it take for you? What would help you reject it?

How has the enemy brought sadness into your relationship with God and the living of your vocation? Can you put words to the sadness he brings? In what particular ways do you find yourself susceptible to this sadness? What can help you reject this sadness?

In what form have you heard insinuations of the enemy—for example, "You'll never be . . . You won't be able to . . . You'll always fail in . . . You know you won't persevere . . ."? In what settings do you hear them? Name the ways you experience the enemy's obstacle-placing action. Again, what can help you reject this?

In what circumstances do you find yourself "figuring it all out" and sinking into discouragement? In such

times, how does the enemy attempt to disquiet you with
false reasons? Name the false reasons. Plan, with the
Lord, how to reject them.

CHAPTER 4

Five Tactics
of the Good Spirit

Can you not do what these men and
women do? . . . Cast yourself upon God
and have no fear. He will not shrink away
and let you fall.

St. Augustine, *Confessions*

We turn now to the work of grace in those
who love God and strive to "rise from
good to better" in God's service. For Ignatius, the
final word is always grace and redemption. I have
always loved this dimension of these rules: they
express a spirituality of redemption, with a pro-
found and happy awareness of God's "sufficient

49

grace" (rule 7) that helps us "resist all our enemies" (rule 11) on the spiritual journey. If the enemy is at work in those growing toward God (rule 2, first part), God's grace is much more at work, strengthening them in this growth (rule 2, second part).

Ignatius names several ways in which the good spirit aids those who seek to rise spiritually. In such persons, he says, the good spirit will "*give courage and strength, consolations, tears, inspirations and quiet, easing and taking away all obstacles.*" As with the first part of rule 2, we will examine and exemplify these tactics.

"Courage and Strength"

When one making the Ignatian retreat is desolate and struggles with temptation, Ignatius writes that his director should not be severe with him but gentle, "giving him *courage and strength* to go forward" (*SpirEx* 7). Ignatius employs precisely the same vocabulary here to describe the work of the good spirit in those growing toward God. In such persons, he affirms, it is proper to the good spirit "to give *courage and strength*."[12]

When St. Augustine feels helpless to break his attachment to sin, the good spirit, portrayed as the virtue of Continence personified, "smiled at me to give me courage."[13] This loving and encouraging action of the good spirit assists St. Augustine finally to break the "chain" that bound him to sin.

A woman who loves the Lord rises one morning and walks down the corridor to put on coffee and begin the day. This afternoon she will meet with the doctor to get the results of the biopsy. Understandably, she is afraid. As she passes along the corridor, her eye catches a placard she has placed on the wall with the parable of the "Footprints in the Sand."[14] Just for a moment, as she passes, the meaning of the parable speaks to her heart: in our times of burden, God is close, carrying us safely through the trial. Her heart lifts, and she knows that the Lord will be with her this day in all that may happen. The good spirit, in a thousand creative ways, gives courage and strength to those who love the Lord.

A woman, active in the Church in her own country, immigrated to a new nation. She joined the local parish and sought her customary involvement in it. Parish life there, however, was so culturally different that she found this increasingly difficult. Finally, at Mass one Sunday, she could bear it no longer When the readings began, she rose, walked down the aisle, and started down the front steps of the church; she was leaving and would never return. At that moment, in God's providence, a woman arrived late for Mass and walked up the steps. As they passed, the woman entering smiled at the woman leaving. The woman leaving stopped, turned around, and went back into the church. When she shared this story, she had been a leader in that parish for forty years. Again, in endlessly creative ways, the good spirit gives courage and strength to those who love and seek God.

A man who sincerely sought God was engaged in a journey of conversion. Along the way, he found himself struggling spiritually. At the time, he was living in New York City, and he describes what followed: "Evening after evening I went to St. Patrick's Roman Catholic Cathedral on Fifth Avenue and spent an hour there praying to God for help and guidance. I liked it there. It was as if the cathedral spoke to me in a quiet, unfaltering voice. It seemed to say, 'Be patient. God will lead you. There are dark nights in every soul—dark nights that precede the dawn. Persevere—don't give up. Stay close to God in doubt and darkness. He will bring you through it.' It was in this assurance that I got through the summer."[15] Here, too, the good spirit gives "courage and strength" to one pursuing growth toward God.

What of our own stories? How have we experienced this encouraging and strengthening action of the good spirit when we needed it to grow in our spiritual lives?

"Consolations"

At times, the good spirit stirs in such persons' hearts a lively awareness of God's closeness and love.

Then their hearts grow warm with God's love, and the joy of this experience engenders new spiritual energy. Ignatius calls such experiences *consolation*.

Some examples will illustrate this. In her journal entry for June 27, 1916, Raïssa Maritain, wife of the philosopher Jacques Maritain, describes her experience in prayer that morning. She begins to pray the Litany of the Sacred Heart of Jesus and never moves beyond the first words, "*Kyrie eleison*: Lord, have mercy." She writes:

> At the first invocation, *Kyrie eleison*, obliged to absorb myself, my mind arrested on the Person of the Father. Impossible to change the object. Sweetness, attraction, *eternal youth* of the heavenly Father. Suddenly, keen sense of his nearness, of his tenderness, of his incomprehensible love which impels him to demand our love, our thought. Greatly moved, I wept very sweet tears. . . . Joy of being able to call him Father with a great tenderness, to feel him so kind and so close to me.[16]

A warm uplift of heart, a blessed sense of God's closeness and love, joy, and the tears that express it: Raïssa is experiencing a blessed consolation from God.

A woman prays daily with Scripture, and today her text is the healing of the woman with the hemorrhage (Mk 5:25–34). She reads through the text attentively a first time, but nothing speaks to her in any particular way. She rereads the text slowly. She notes how this woman hopes for healing but only as an anonymous brush of a finger in a crowd. The woman does touch Jesus's garments and is healed. But now Jesus asks who touched him. The disciples make the obvious comment about the press of the crowd, but Jesus knows, and the woman knows.

As the woman prays with this scene, she sees this woman, now healed, come with great courage, fall down before Jesus, and tell him the whole truth. As she prays, she hears Jesus's first word of response, "Daughter," which tells the woman that she is much more for him than an anonymous brush of a finger in a crowd but that a deep and beautiful relationship is established between them. As the woman praying perceives Jesus's response, her heart is warmed with an awareness that Jesus says the same to her, "Daughter," and that he loves her, too, with all the richness this word signifies. She is experiencing a gentle and rich spiritual consolation.

All of us, in our individual ways, have experienced such consolations, and we rightly recognize them for the gifts that they are. Through them, the good spirits encourage us to move ahead on the path of growth.

"Tears"

Tears may express varied sentiments. These tears, a gift of the good spirit, are blessed tears, the body's sharing in the heart's awareness of God's love, closeness, protection, and guidance.

A man rises and goes to church this morning. He arrives thirty minutes before Mass and dedicates the time, according to his habitual practice, to prayer with the day's Gospel. He is tired and discouraged because of problems at work and at home. The church is large, cold, and almost empty at this early hour.

This day's Gospel is the encounter of Jesus with the disciples on the way to Emmaus (Lk 24:13–35). As the man reads this text, he sees these two disciples, whose hearts are sad and who have lost hope, quietly leave the community. He notes how Jesus approaches them, listens to them, and speaks with them. He watches their "slow" hearts become "burning" hearts (Lk 24:25, 32). Then they reach the village, and Jesus appears to be traveling further. The man hears the prayer of these two disciples, a prayer he, too, has often made to the Lord, "Stay with us! Darkness is falling" (see Lk 24:29). He sees how Jesus welcomes that prayer, goes in with them, and their lives are changed forever. As the man reads this, the beginning of a tear comes to his eye: "Lord, you are with me, too, in my tiredness and discouragement. You hear my prayer when I call out to you in my need."

The woman who enters the Pharisee's house never says a word but expresses everything with her tears (Lk 7:36–50). Her tears are tears of consolation. They are blessed and healing tears that express her heart's awareness that, perhaps for the first time in her life, she is welcomed, respected, understood, loved, and set free for a new life. These are beautiful experiences of consoling and strengthening tears. All of us, in our varied situations, have experienced such tears, and we rightly treasure the grace that inspires them.

"Inspirations and Quiet"

The enemy brings *false reasons* to the mind that *disquiet* the heart; the good spirit brings *inspirations* to the mind and *quiet*—that is, peace—to the heart. Here Ignatius highlights a cognitive dimension in the good spirit's action: such *inspirations* bring clarity to the person and reveal the steps to be taken. Likewise, the good spirit instills a warm *quiet* of heart—the rest, as St. Augustine writes, that our restless hearts seek.

Earlier we spoke of Gerald at Sunday Mass and the homily on Luke 11:1–13, "Lord, teach us to pray." When the priest invites his parishioners to pray for ten minutes with the daily readings from Mass, the good spirit brings inspirations to Gerald: "If simply praying once a week at Sunday Mass is already making this difference, what would happen if I . . . prayed daily?. . . I could certainly arrange my morning to set aside ten minutes each day. And . . . all I have to do is ask my wife for help because she has been doing this for some years." The good spirit gives clarity—inspirations—to Gerald regarding the next steps to be taken. As we review our spiritual journeys, all of us will recognize this action of the good spirit. Through the words or example of a friend, a spouse, or a spiritual guide; through a sermon; through prayer with Scripture or before the Blessed Sacrament; and in many other ways, the good spirit has shown us the way to "go forward in doing good."

"Easing and Taking Away All Obstacles"

In those rising toward God, the enemy *places obstacles*; in such persons, the good spirit *eases and takes away all obstacles*. The word *all* expresses Ignatius's confidence that, with the aid of the good spirit, *every* obstacle on this path toward growth can be overcome.

Let us return once more to Gerald's experience, now later on that same Sunday after the grace-filled Mass. The conversation at supper with his teenage son does not resolve well, and Gerald is discouraged as the evening unfolds. Now his thoughts about beginning the ten minutes with Scripture are different: "You've been away from the Church for twenty years. . . . You've never even read Scripture. What makes you think you'll understand anything written there? Why approach your wife about a practice that is bound to fail? You'll just embarrass yourself and her." The enemy *places obstacles* in the way of one who is seeking to rise from good to better in God's service.

Burdened by these obstacles, Gerald is at the point of relinquishing this new step. Then his eight-year-old daughter comes into his study to say good night. She hugs him and says, "I love you." Gerald returns her hug and says, "I love you, too." Something in Gerald's heart lifts, and when she leaves the room, he resolves, "I will speak this evening with my wife as I planned this morning, and I will begin the prayer tomorrow." Through the love of his daughter, the good spirit has *eased and taken away all obstacles* to this next step in Gerald's spiritual growth.

The Strengthening Tactics of the Good Spirit: Some Examples

I take these examples, like those of the preceding chapter, from my journals. They describe ways in which I have experienced the encouraging action of the good spirit.

"This Brings Peace and Hope"

I wrote the following in a time of physical difficulty that required me to cancel most of my ministry. This page describes the conclusions of my examen prayer[17] one evening:

I see two different approaches to my situation. One approach says, "It's over. You won't do any more ministry. And it's your fault." This voice brings fear, depression, and desolation.

The other approach says, "God's love is at work in all of this, giving you time to rest, to pray, to make progress on your writing, keeping you from the danger of trying to do too much. The future is in God's hands, and he loves you. The Father gives good things to those who ask (Mt 7:11)." This brings peace and hope.

The first approach is the lie of the enemy. The second is the good spirit.

I was struck that evening by the contrariety of two different perceptions of the same experience: the discouraging lies of the enemy and the action of the good spirit giving "courage and strength." I knew that I would bring this to spiritual direction in my next meeting.

"I Find an Uplift of Heart"

The Virgin Mary has often been the "instrument" of the good spirit in giving me courage and strength. On one day of struggle:

> Again, Mary, you lift my heart, and I experience consolation in the midst of tiredness, feeling too alone, and concern for the writing I am doing. I ask for your help with all of this, and I find an uplift of heart. You are a space of the good spirit for me.

And after finishing an eight-day Ignatian retreat:

> Mary is the answer to the insinuations of the enemy that the newness of the retreat will fade, that things will go back as they were before, that this grace will be lost. When I turn to you, Mary, I feel that this is just beginning, that it will grow. I feel "courage and strength."

"Why Would God Ever Not Want You to Go to Mass?"

I share the following with the permission of the narrator:

I was raised Catholic and had a good education in the faith, but I had been away from the Church for years. Then I met my future wife. On our first date, we walked together around a lake. As we were parting, I asked, "Will I see you again?" She answered, "You can come to Mass with me this Sunday." I didn't know how to answer, and I said that I would get back to her.

That night I struggled until 2:00 a.m., unable to sleep, going back and forth, not knowing what to do. I felt that I couldn't go to Mass. Finally, at 2:00 a.m., the thought came to me, "Why don't you pray?" I got down on my knees and tried to pray.

A thought came to me: "You are just using Mass for a date. You can't do that." Then another thought came to me: "Why would God ever *not* want you to go to Mass, whatever the reason?" That was my answer. I went back to bed, fell asleep, and went with her to Mass that Sunday. It was the beginning of my return to the Church.

The *inspirations* of the good spirit in one considering, however hesitantly, new steps toward God are evident in this account. The first was the invitation to pray; the second, the question "Why would God ever *not* want you to go to Mass, whatever the reason?" When the young man acts on both inspirations, he does indeed "go forward in doing good."

"I Don't Know Why I'm So Moved"

This was one of those airplane conversations, and I have never forgotten it. The woman seated next to me told me that she was about to go to Mass for the first time in ten years. She explained that she was raised Catholic but had been away from the Church at length. She said that her studies in medical school were nearly complete, that she had always been successful, but for the first time was facing failure. I sensed the heaviness in her heart as she asked, "Yet how can I return to God? For years, when all was well, I ignored him. Now just because I need something, I'm planning to go back to Mass. How can I go to God this way?" A comment: such considerations are classic instances of the enemy's obstacle-placing action in one seeking to move toward God.

I asked her if she knew the parable of the prodigal son, and she said that she did not. I explained that when the son returns, his motive is centered on his own need, but that is all the father needs. The father runs, draws near, embraces his son, kisses him, and celebrates his return with joy. This parable brought tears to her eyes, and I saw the light and hope it awakened in her. She said, "I don't know why I'm so moved."

I felt that I knew why. Through the power of the Scriptures, the good spirit *eased and took away all obstacles* so that she might go forward on her new journey toward God.

Questions for Reflection

Review your experience of the good spirit's five tactics. Thank God for the love he shows you through them. Prepare your heart to receive them in the future.

In what ways has the Lord given you courage? Given you strength to go forward in the spiritual life? Through what persons, reading, digital resources, events, ways of praying? How can you continue to benefit from these sources of strength?

Can you name one or more experiences of spiritual consolation—times when you felt the Lord's love and closeness, perhaps even to tears? When did these occur? What grace did God give you through them? Remember, and give thanks to God. Open your heart to receive any future consolations the Lord may give.

Think back to inspirations you have received from the Lord, times when you saw the next step, when you saw clearly where the Lord was leading. What fruits arose from these inspirations? Ask the Lord for openness to the inspirations he may wish to give.

How have you experienced the obstacle-removing action of the good spirit? Can you remember times when it just seemed too difficult, that you couldn't go forward, when you were ready to give up—and the good spirit eased the path through prayer, the Eucharist, the words of a friend, a homily, the smile of another? Let your heart expand in gratitude to the God who opens the way and gives you all you need.

CHAPTER 5

Finding the Path to Freedom

He has sent me to proclaim liberty to captives
and . . . to let the oppressed go free.

Luke 4:18

In his rule 2, Ignatius helps us understand the four tactics of the enemy as the discouraging lies that they are: his *biting*, attempts to *sadden* us, *placing of obstacles* in our way, and *disquieting* of our hearts with *false reasons*. There is no shame in experiencing these tactics of the enemy. I repeat this because of its importance: There is no shame in experiencing these tactics of the enemy! We all do. Everyone who loves the Lord does.

This is simply what it means to live the spiritual life in a fallen, yes, but redeemed and loved world.

What *does* matter is to be aware of these tactics, to identify them in our daily experience, and firmly to reject them for the lies that they are. Then we are no longer captives. Then we are set free (Lk 4:18).

In rule 2, Ignatius also helps us understand the five encouraging tactics of the good spirit: his heartening *courage and strength*, warm *consolations*, blessed *tears*, enlightening *inspirations*, and *easing of all obstacles*. Aware of these tactics, identifying them in our daily experience, and opening our hearts to receive them, we are set free to "go forward in doing good," to love and serve the Lord whose love never leaves us.

Major decisions occur only occasionally in the spiritual life. The most significant is our vocational choice. On other levels, pivotal points may arise from time to time. The greater part of the spiritual life, however, is lived on the daily level, with its ebb and flow of spiritual energy. The tapestry of our spiritual lives is woven through the many decisions we make each day, when we reject the enemy's discouragements and open our hearts to God's encouraging interventions. It is precisely on this daily level that Ignatius's rule 2 brings clarity and hope.

That is why rule 2 is so important and of such great benefit. May it be for us, as it has for so many, a source of freedom on the spiritual journey.

The Text of the Fourteen Rules
Literal Translation

Rules for becoming aware and understanding to some extent the different movements which are caused in the soul, the good, to receive them, and the bad to reject them. And these rules are more proper for the first week.

First Rule. The first rule: in persons who are going from mortal sin to mortal sin, the enemy is ordinarily accustomed to propose apparent pleasures to them, leading them to imagine sensual delights and pleasures in order to hold them more and make them grow in their vices and sins. In these persons the good spirit uses a contrary method, stinging and biting their consciences through their rational power of moral judgment.

Second Rule. The second: in persons who are going on intensely purifying their sins and rising from good to better in the service of God our Lord, the method is contrary to that in the first rule. For then it is proper to the evil spirit to bite, sadden, and place obstacles, disquieting with false reasons, so that the person may not go forward. And it is proper to the good spirit to give courage and strength, consolations, tears, inspirations and quiet, easing and taking away all obstacles, so that the person may go forward in doing good.

Third Rule. The third is of spiritual consolation. I call it consolation when some interior movement is caused in the soul, through which the soul comes to be inflamed with love of its Creator and Lord, and, consequently when it can love no created thing on the face of the earth in itself, but only in the Creator of them all. Likewise when it sheds tears that move to love of its Lord, whether out of sorrow for one's sins, or for the passion of Christ our Lord, or because of other things directly ordered to his service and praise. Finally, I call consolation every increase of hope, faith and charity, and all interior joy that calls and attracts to heavenly things and to the salvation of one's soul, quieting it and giving it peace in its Creator and Lord.

Fourth Rule. The fourth is of spiritual desolation. I call desolation all the contrary of the third rule, such as darkness of soul, disturbance in it, movement to low and earthly things, disquiet from various agitations and temptations, moving to lack of confidence, without hope, without love, finding oneself totally slothful, tepid, sad and, as if separated from one's Creator and Lord. For just as consolation is contrary to desolation, in the same way the thoughts that come from consolation are contrary to the thoughts that come from desolation.

Fifth Rule. The fifth: in time of desolation never make a change, but be firm and constant in the proposals and determination in which one was the day preceding such desolation, or in the determination in which one was in the preceding consolation. Because, as in consolation the good spirit guides and counsels us more, so in desolation the bad spirit, with whose counsels we cannot find the way to a right decision.

Sixth Rule. The sixth: although in desolation we should not change our first proposals, it is very advantageous to change ourselves intensely against the desolation itself, as by insisting more upon prayer, meditation, upon much examination, and upon extending ourselves in some suitable way of doing penance.

Seventh Rule. The seventh: let one who is in desolation consider how the Lord has left him in trial in his natural powers, so that he may resist the various agitations and temptations of the enemy; since he can resist with the divine help, which always remains with him, though he does not clearly feel it; for the Lord has taken away from him his great fervor, abundant love and intense grace, leaving him, however, sufficient grace for eternal salvation.

Eighth Rule. The eighth: let one who is in desolation work to be in patience, which is contrary to the vexations which come to him, and let him think that he will soon be consoled, diligently using the means against such desolation, as is said in the sixth rule.

Ninth Rule. The ninth: there are three principal causes for which we find ourselves desolate. The first is because we are tepid, slothful or negligent in our spiritual exercises, and so through our faults spiritual consolation withdraws from us. The second, to try us and see how much we are and how much we extend ourselves in his service and praise without so much payment of consolations and increased graces. The third, to give us true recognition and understanding so that we may interiorly feel that it is not ours to attain or maintain increased devotion, intense love, tears or any other spiritual consolation, but that all is the gift and grace of God our Lord, and so that we may not build a nest in something belonging to another, raising our mind in some pride or vainglory, attributing to ourselves the devotion or the other parts of the spiritual consolation.

Tenth Rule. The tenth: let the one who is in consolation think how he will conduct himself in the desolation which will come after, taking new strength for that time.

Eleventh Rule. The eleventh: let one who is consoled seek to humble himself and lower himself as much as he can, thinking of how little he is capable in the time of desolation without such grace or consolation. On the contrary, let one who is in desolation think that he can do much with God's sufficient grace to resist all his enemies, taking strength in his Creator and Lord.

Twelfth Rule. The twelfth: the enemy acts like a woman in being weak when faced with strength and strong when faced with weakness. For, as it is proper to a woman, when she is fighting with some man, to lose heart and to flee when the man confronts her firmly, and, on the contrary, if the man begins to flee, losing heart, the anger, vengeance and ferocity of the woman grow greatly and know no bounds, in the same way, it is proper to the enemy to weaken and lose heart, fleeing and ceasing his temptations when the person who is exercising himself in spiritual things confronts the temptations of the enemy firmly, doing what is diametrically opposed to them; and, on the contrary, if the person who is exercising himself begins to be afraid and lose heart in suffering the temptations, there is no beast so fierce on the face of the earth as the enemy of human nature in following out his damnable intention with such growing malice.

Thirteenth Rule. The thirteenth: likewise he conducts himself as a false lover in wishing to remain secret and not be revealed. For a dissolute man who, speaking with evil intention, makes dishonorable advances to a daughter of a good father or a wife of a good husband, wishes his words and persuasions to be secret, and the contrary displeases him very much, when the daughter reveals to her father or the wife to her husband his false words and depraved intention, because he easily perceives that he will not be able to succeed with the undertaking begun. In the same way, when the enemy of human nature brings his wiles and persuasions to the just soul, he wishes and desires that they be received and kept in secret; but when one reveals them to one's good confessor or to another spiritual person, who knows his deceits and malicious designs, it weighs on him very much, because he perceives that he will not be able to succeed with the malicious undertaking he has begun, since his manifest deceits have been revealed.

Fourteenth Rule. The fourteenth: likewise he conducts himself as a leader, intent upon conquering and robbing what he desires. For, just as a captain and leader of an army in the field, pitching his camp and exploring the fortifications and defenses of a stronghold, attacks it at the weakest point, in the same way the enemy of human nature, roving about, looks in turn at all our theological, cardinal and moral virtues; and where he finds us weakest and most in need for our eternal salvation, there he attacks us and attempts to take us.

The Text of the Fourteen Rules
Contemporary Version

1. When a person lives a life of serious sin, the enemy fills the imagination with images of sensual pleasures; the good spirit stings and bites in the person's conscience, God's loving action, calling the person back.

2. When you try to avoid sin and to love God, this reverses: now the enemy tries to bite, discourage, and sadden; the good spirit gives you courage and strength, inspirations, easing the path forward.

3. When your heart finds joy in God, a sense of God's closeness and love, you are experiencing spiritual consolation. Open your heart to God's gift!

4. When your heart is discouraged, you have little energy for spiritual things, and God feels far away, you are experiencing spiritual desolation. Resist and reject this tactic of enemy!

5. "In time of desolation, never make a change!" When you are in spiritual desolation, never change anything in your spiritual life.

6. When you are in spiritual desolation, use these four means: prayer (ask God's help!), meditation (think of Bible verses, truths about God's faithful love, memories of God's fidelity to you in the past), examination (ask, "What am I feeling? How did this start?"), and suitable penance (don't just give in and immerse

yourself in social media, music, movies . . .).
Stand your ground in suitable ways!

7. When you are in spiritual desolation, *think*
of this truth: God is giving me all the grace I
need to get safely through this desolation.

8. When you are in spiritual desolation, be
patient, stay the course, and remember that
consolation will return much sooner than the
desolation is telling you.

9. Why does a God who loves us allow us to
experience spiritual desolation? To help us see
changes we need to make; to strengthen us in
our resistance to desolation; and to help us
not get complacent in the spiritual life.

10. When you are in spiritual consolation, remember that desolation will return at some point,
and prepare for it.

11. The mature person of discernment: neither carelessly high in consolation nor despairingly low in desolation, but humble in consolation and trusting in desolation.

12. Resist the enemy's temptations right at their very beginning. This is when it is easiest.

13. When you find burdens on your heart in your spiritual life, temptations, confusion, discouragement, find a wise, competent spiritual person and talk about it.

14. Identify that area of your life where you are most vulnerable to the enemy's temptations and discouraging lies, and strengthen it.

Notes

1. Timothy M. Gallagher, OMV, *Setting Captives Free: Personal Reflections on Ignatian Discernment of Spirits* (New York: Crossroad, 2018).

2. Ignatius also composed a second set of eight rules for discernment (*SpirEx* 328–336). These rules deal with questions of discernment beyond the scope of this book. For this second set of rules, see Timothy M. Gallagher, OMV, *Spiritual Consolation: An Ignatian Guide for the Greater Discernment of Spirits* (New York: Crossroad, 2006).

3. Dorothy Day, *The Long Loneliness* (San Francisco: Harper & Row, 1952), 10.

4. For the text of this rule, see the appendices.

5. Author's translation. See Timothy M. Gallagher, OMV, *The Discernment of Spirits: An Ignatian Guide to Everyday Living* (New York: Crossroad, 2005), 7.

6. Ignatius to Sister Teresa Rejadell, 18 June 1536, in William Young, SJ, *Letters of Saint Ignatius of*

Loyola (Chicago: Loyola University Press, 1959), 21. Emphasis added.

7. *Autobiography*, para. 22. Author's translation from the original in Manuel Ruiz Jurado, SJ, ed., San Ignacio de Loyola: Obras (Madrid: Biblioteca de Autores Cristianos, 2013), 42.

8. Ignatius to Sister Teresa Rejadell. See Timothy M. Gallagher, OMV, *Discernment of Spirits*, 40.

9. R. S. Pine-Coffin, trans., *Saint Augustine: Confessions* (Harmondsworth, UK: Penguin Books, 1961), 8.11, pp. 175–76. See Gallagher, *Discernment of Spirits*, 29.

10. Leo Tolstoy, *Resurrection*, trans. Rosemary Edmonds (London: Penguin, 1966), 141. See Gallagher, *Discernment of Spirits*, 194n6.

11. *Ascent of Mount Carmel*, 1.12.6, in Kieran Kavanaugh, OCD, and Otilio Rodriguez, OCD, trans., *The Collected Works of St. John of the Cross* (Washington, DC: ICS Publications, 1991), 147.

12. *dándole ánimo y fuerzas* (*SpirEx* 7); *dar ánimo y fuerzas* (*SpirEx* 315).

13. Pine-Coffin, *Saint Augustine: Confessions*, 8.11, p. 176.

14. The following are the concluding words of this lovely message: "The Lord replied, my precious, precious child, I love you and I would never leave you! During your times of trial and suffering when you see only one set of footprints, it was then that I carried you." See www.wowzone.com/fprints.htm.

15. William Kernan, *My Road to Certainty* (New York: D. McKay Co., 1953), 63.

16. Jacques Maritain, ed., *Raïssa's Journal* (Albany, NY: Magi Books, 1974), 35. See Gallagher, *Discernment of Spirits*, 47. For a complete treatment of spiritual consolation, see Gallagher, *Discernment of Spirits*, 47–57, and *Setting Captives Free*, 45–66.

17. The examen prayer is an Ignatian exercise of prayer in which people review their spiritual experience of the day. See Timothy Gallagher, OMV, *The Examen Prayer: Ignatian Wisdom for Our Lives Today* (New York: Crossroad, 2006).

Resources

In this book, we have focused on one of Ignatius's fourteen rules. Obviously, much more might be said about them! I list here three books that I have written on them:

The Discernment of Spirits: An Ignatian Guide to Everyday Living. New York: Crossroad, 2005.

Setting Captives Free: Personal Reflections on Ignatian Discernment of Spirits. New York: Crossroad, 2018.

A Reader's Guide to The Discernment of Spirits: An Ignatian Guide to Everyday Living. New York: Crossroad, 2013.

About the Author

Father Timothy M. Gallagher, OMV, was ordained in 1979 as a member of the Oblates of the Virgin Mary, a religious community dedicated to retreats and spiritual formation according to the Spiritual Exercises of St. Ignatius. Having obtained his doctorate in 1983 from the Gregorian University, he has taught (St. John's Seminary, Brighton, Massachusetts; Our Lady of Grace Seminary Residence, Boston, Massachusetts), assisted in formation work, and served two terms as provincial in his own community. He has dedicated many years to an extensive international ministry of retreats, spiritual direction, and teaching about the spiritual life. He is a frequent speaker on EWTN, and his digitally recorded talks are utilized internationally. He has written many books on Ignatian discernment and prayer; on the life and spiritual teaching of Venerable Bruno Lanteri, founder of the Oblates; and on the Liturgy of the Hours. He currently holds the St. Ignatius Chair for Spiritual Formation at St. John Vianney Theological Seminary in Denver.

Which Ignatian Title is Right for You?

Timothy Gallagher, OMV

Hundreds of thousands of readers are turning to Fr. Gallagher's Ignatian titles for reliable, inspirational, and clear explanations of some of the most important aspects of Christian spirituality. Whether you're a spiritual director, priest, or minister, longtime spiritual seeker, or beginner, Fr. Gallagher's books have much to offer you in different moments in life.

When you need short, practical exercises for young and old:

An Ignatian Introduction to Prayer

Group leaders who are looking for practical exercise for groups, including groups who may not have much experience in spiritual development, will want to acquire *An Ignatian Introduction to Prayer: Scriptural Reflections According to the Spiritual Exercises.* This book features forty short (two-page) Ignatian mediations, including Scripture passages, meditative keys for entering into the scriptural story, and guided questions for reflection. These exercises are also useful for individual reflection, both for experienced persons and beginners; beginners will recognize and resonate with some of the evocative passages from Scripture; those familiar with Ignatian teaching will appreciate the Ignatian structure of the guided questions.

Ignatian Introduction to Prayer	Paperback 9780824524876	EPUB 9780824521905
		Mobipocket 9780824521912

When you seek a short, accessible introduction to Ignatius's teaching on how to respond to struggles in the daily spiritual life:

When You Struggle in the Spiritual Life:
An Ignatian Path to Freedom

This book, through clear explanations and many practical examples, will introduce you to Ignatius's rules for the discernment of spirits. It focuses on the rule (the second) that clarifies the spiritual experience of those who love God, seek to live accordingly—and who struggle.

When You Struggle in the Spiritual Life   Paperback 9780824597023

When your life is at the crossroads:

Discerning the Will of God

If you're facing a turning point in life, you know how difficult it can be to try to hear God's will amid the noise of other people's expectations and your own wishes. Ignatius of Loyola developed a series of exercises and reflections designed to help you in these times so that your decision can be one that conforms to God's will for your life. *Discerning the Will of God: An Ignatian Guide to Christian Decision Making* is a trustworthy guide to applying those reflections to your own particular circumstances. This guide, which does not require any prior knowledge of Ignatian spirituality, can be used by people of any faith, though some elements will be more directly applicable to Catholic readers. This book is widely used and is the basis of a television series.

Discerning the Will of God   Paperback 9780824524890   EPUB 9780824526399
                          Mobipocket 9780824526405   DVD Video 9780824520335   CD 9780824520274

When you want classic spiritual discipline to apply every day:

The Examen Prayer and *Meditation and Contemplation*

Individuals wanting to deepen their prayer lives using a spiritual discipline will find *The Examen Prayer* an important resource. The examen prayer is a powerful and increasingly popular resource for finding God's hand in our everyday lives and learning to be receptive to God's blessings. This easy-to-read book uses stories and examples to explain what the examen is, how you can begin to pray it, how you can adapt it to your individual life, and what its benefits for your life can be. Highly practical!

Because *The Examen Prayer* draws from the experiences of everyday life, it can stand on its own as a guide to the prayer of examen. Those looking to begin their practice of meditation and contemplation, which for Ignatius is always based on Scripture, may choose their own Scripture passages or draw from the forty examples in *An Ignatian Introduction to Prayer*, mentioned earlier.

Examen Prayer		Paperback 9780824523671	EPUB 9780824549725
	Mobipocket 9780824549763	CD 9780824521851	MP3 9780824523251

A second favorite is *Meditation and Contemplation: An Ignatian Guide to Praying with Scripture*. Anyone familiar with Ignatian spirituality has heard about meditation and contemplation. In this volume, Fr. Gallagher explains what is unique to each practice, shows how you can profit from both at different times in your spiritual life, and reveals some of the forgotten elements (such as the preparatory steps and colloquy) and how the structure can be adapted to your particular spiritual needs. This book, like *The Examen Prayer*, has been presented as a television series.

Meditation and Contemplation	Paperback 9780824524883	EPUB 9780824549732
		Mobipocket 9780824549770

The Discernment of Spirits, *Setting Captives Free*, and *Spiritual Consolation*

Spiritual directors, directees, and others who want to understand the deeper structures of Ignatian thought have come to rely on *The Discernment of Spirits: An Ignatian Guide to Everyday Living*. *The Discernment of Spirits* leads us through Ignatius's Rules for discernment, showing both their precise insight into the human soul and their ability to illustrate the real-life struggles of spiritual seekers today. As Fr. Gallagher writes, his practical goal is "to offer an experience-based presentation of Ignatius's rules for discernment of spiritus in order to facilitate their ongoing application in the spiritual life. This is a book abut living the spiritual life." Because it forms the foundation for so many other aspects of Ignatian thought, *The Discernment of Spirits* has become Fr. Gallagher's best-selling book and has been the basis for a television series.

Discernment of Spirits		Paperback 9780824522919	EPUB 9780824549718
	Mobipocket 9780824549756	CD 9780824520045	MP3 9780824523244

Discernment of Spirits: A Reader's Guide	Paperback 9780824549855

Discernimiento de los espiritus	Paperback 9780824522186

In *Setting Captives Free: Personal Reflections on Ignatian Discernment of Spirits*, Fr. Gallagher takes up the content of *The Discernment of Spirits* and explores it further, with further insights into Ignatius's rules and a wealth of additional examples, including many from his own experience.

Setting Captives Free	Paperback 9780824599072	EPUB 9780824599393
		Mobipocket 9780824599409

Spiritual Consolation: An Ignatian Guide for the Greater Discernment of Spirits, utilizes the same, clear, experience-based approach to explain and apply Ignatius's Second Rules for discernment. It brings clarity into the sensitive and complex discernment that Ignatius discusses in these rules.

Spiritual Consolation   Paperback 9780824524296   EPUB 9780824549749
                                                    Mobipocket 9780824549787

When you want to share this Ignatian teaching with others:

A Handbook for Spiritual Directors and *Teaching Discernment*

When spiritual directors are asked to accompany directees as they discern God's will in choices they face, they, the directors, readily turn to Ignatius for guidance in this delicate task. In *A Handbook for Spiritual Directors: An Ignatian Guide for Accompanying Discernment of God's Will*, Fr. Gallagher provides a systematic and clear exposition of Ignatius's teaching, equipping them to assist their directees with competence and confidence.

Handbook for Spiritual Directors	Paperback 9780824521714	EPUB 9780824501440
		Mobipocket 9780824501457

In *Teaching Discernment: A Pedagogy for Presenting Ignatian Discernment of Spirits*, Fr. Gallagher shares the approach to teaching Ignatius's rules for discernment that he has shaped in forty years of ministry. This approach, based on close attention to Ignatius's own words and abundant use of concrete examples, has rendered these rules accessible to thousands throughout the world. This book prepares the readers to share the rules with others in an effective way.

Teaching Discernment	Paperback 9780824599355	EPUB 9780824599713
		Mobipocket 9780824599720

Other Books by Fr. Timothy Gallagher

Praying the Liturgy of the Hours	Paperback 9780824520328	EPUB 9780824520434
		Mobipocket 9780824520458

Begin Again	Paperback 9780824525798	EPUB 9780824520281	Mobipocket 9780824520298